Living With These Broken Wings

Jessica Badrick

Presentation by *BookLeaf Publishing*

Web: www.bookleafpub.com

E-mail: info@bookleafpub.com

ISBN: 9789358310238

First edition 2023

DEDICATION

I dedicate this book to the friends who stuck by my side through the darkness and my lovely pixie who has far better grammatical skills than I could ever dream of.

Indomitable

There's the sting.
Then a pinch.
Next the slice,
Out pours red.
Ah, I am ten feet tall
And bulletproof again.

My armors thick.
My tongue is sharp.
This numb I don't hear others' cruelty.
Riding high,
I am ten feet tall and bulletproof.

Wash the old one,
Man it stings.
Find a new spot,
Press in hard.
That's the pinch.
Then slide down fast,
To make the slice.
Ah, that sweet release, now
I am ten feet tall and bulletproof.

Watch the blood run in a stream,
Feel all the tension leave.

Numb the bullying and abuse,
Let the trapped thoughts fly loose.
For now
I am ten feet tall and bulletproof,
Again!

Tick Tick Tick

Tick. Tick. Tick.
It's all I hear,
It just won't stop!
Tick. Tick. Tick.
Its sound so loud I suffocate,
It just won't stop!
Tick. Tick. Tick.
It's my only thought
It just won't stop!
Tick! Tick! Tick!
The pressure, it's amplified!
Tick! Tick! Tick!
It just won't stop!
Tick! Tick! Tick!
I'm like a bomb about to blow!
TICK. TICK. TOCK!
Finally, I just made it stop.

Breathe

Step one:
Take a breath.
Step two:
Take another breath.
Step three:
Repeat one and two.
I can't keep this up.
I feel like I am drowning.
How can this be the right way,
When everything feels so wrong?
One little slice and I wouldn't feel a thing.
Step one:
Take a breath.
Step two:
Take another breath.
Step three:
Repeat one and two.
Maybe people don't realize
How easily they could stop this.
I can't imagine everyone enjoys this.
My skin crawls!
It's too loud!
Too bright!
Too close!
They all make it look so easy!

Step one:
Take a breath.
Step two:
Take another breath.
Step three:
Repeat one and two.

Never Ending Relapsing

One day
One minute
One second
I got this.
I can do this?
I don't need it.
Take a breath.
I can do this.
I am stronger?
I can beat this craving.
Block them out!
Close my eyes.
Take a breath.
I can do this.
Push away the panic and the doubt.
I can do this?
Start with a second...
Then a mintue....
Then an hour....
Then just one
Ooops!

Baby Steps

I got this!
We set a goal:
One month.
I can do this!
Take a breath.
Take a break.
Know my limits.
I got this?
Nope, I don't have this.
Skin's crawling!
Ears pounding!
Can't breathe!
It's too bright.
Too close.
Too quiet.
Too loud.
Can't focus!
NO!
STOP!
Take a breath!
Take a break!
Walk away!
Phew, I made it through today!
I did it!
I made one whole day!

Solid Progress

Three months clean.
Look at me go!
I've been doing great.
Everyone's so proud of me
But today was bad.
The pull is way too strong.
My ears pound.
The tensions thick.
I know I shouldn't but.
Just one slice ...
One little nick...
No I can't start again
I can't backslide.
Maybe if I just
Try to hide.
Put my headphones on.
Stay in my room out of site.
Nope!
No being invisible tonight.
Try to block it out.
Try to breathe.
Ignore the craving.
Ignore the pressure.
I have to do this,
Everyone's counting on me!

Back Slide

Oh no this is bad
I had made a whole six months.
Maybe I can hide this
After just one more.
Is there even a spot for one more?
There's a lot of blood.
Maybe I should tell someone?
NO!
No, I can't they wouldn't understand.
I failed them again.
I just keep proving
I am the awful things they call me.
How can I hide this,
It's my whole upper arm.
That's not skin It's raw flesh and blood.
Do they even make band-aids or gause patches
this big?

Turning Point.

Look how tiny he is.
Look how he looks at me.
No judgment.
No contempt.
Nothing but pure love and trust.
Why would they leave him with me?
This helpless little thing.
His whole life depending on me.
I don't know what I am doing?
Why trust me with raising him?
Never mind look at them.
Oh boy, he needs me.
Guess I am quitting cold turkey?
No failure this time!
This cutting thing has to stop!

She Said Not the Same But...

Yes, no, yes.
Confusion!
That look, that smile; they say yes.
That action, that comment; they say no.
That hug, that text they; say yes.
It's ok here but not there.
I have done this before.
I was a secret before.
I could do this again,
But do I want to?
I thought I had finally
Found real...
But now you make no sense.
Now you're acting like the rest.
Is this actually real?

Where Do I Stand

Where do I stand?
You say one thing and do another,
Words and actions barely matching.
It's ok in front of them but not them.
Your yes means no and your no means no
And all I've known for these six years is
Confusion.
I am good either way,
But this
Confusion fog is killing me.
I can feel my soul dying,
One neuron at a time.

Statistics

Why lie about it?
I am not a China doll.
Twenty years of "friendship".
And 6 in "love".
If you don't feel the same, tell me!
Why lie?
Don't say it's ok when it's not.
Don't let me form patterned
Routines you don't want.
Rumors start with truths,
I should have seen it coming.
Why did I think I could have happiness.
Just tell the truth!
This confusion land
Was overrated long before
You asked me out.
I'd rather be told no,
Than have my soul ripped out.
I should have known.
Story of my life.
Statistics show happiness
Will never be mine.

Obscured

It's you!
No, me?
Wait, is it you plus me?
What to do,
What to say.
Was it right?
Wait I know, it was wrong.
I doubt myself,
I doubt you too.
Do I change my mind?
Change the words?
Maybe I'll change the whole act.
Can I tell what's real and true?
Will you help me see the truth?
Fake, phony, just untrue.
All the things, I
Think about you.
Do you think the same of me?
I speak the truth.
Speak in turn.
But I know it's all you.
Now, can I say it?
The right thing,
Right words,
Right thoughts too?

Just tell me the truth!
Was it me?
Was it you?
Was it really all wrong,
You plus me?

A Solution

Can I really do this?
It seems too easy.
And yet at the same time,
It's a terrifying summit of
Unsurmountable fear.
It's been so long
She burnt me so bad
I still can't trust anyone.
Even to make friends,
Let alone more.
Just the thought of it,
I feel like I am suffocating.
Chest tightens,
Words freeze,
Palms sweat.
Life goes forward.
It won't stop just for me.
I can't trust so,
I just won't ever fall in love again.

Insanity

It's been so long,
I had given up.
I swore I was never going to love again.
But look at those eyes and that smile.
They compliment that gorgeous soul so well.
I'm so unsure.
I don't even remember how this goes.
What if she says no.
I am pretty sure she can hear my heart pounding
Through my chest.
She just smiled, was that at me?
I feel like a teen on my first date.
I don't think this could go any worse

Crack in the Armor

I didn't ask for this.
I tried so hard.
I fought the feelings.
Told them no.
I know this will be bad.
It ends the same way every time,
Statistics prove it so.
How could my brain let my heart take control.
We Have been down this road before. It is never
good. A horrible battle, I never seem to win.
No! No! No!
I didn't ask for this!
The pros and cons just don't add up.
She could never love me.
Statistics show I can not trust.
And yet she has not left.
She has not run.
NO! NO! NO!
Stop this foolishness!
Don't think maybe.
Don't get hopes up.
She could never love me.
I can not trust.
I have nothing left to give,
I am already broken,

Damaged goods.
She's still there,
Still standing here.
Looking at me.
Waiting for me.
Maybe I can try.

Hope

It's been a few weeks,
She's still here.
I don't know why, but
She's still here.
I've been me and,
She's still here.
I've been angry and,
She's still here.
I've been anxious and insecure but,
She's still here.
Could it be?
Could she really mean it,
when she says she loves me?

Game On

I push you pull
I pull you push
This tug of war of my soul,
Is a game only I enjoy.
I don't trust and I am mean.
Never had a reason not to be obscene.
You are kind and gentle
With open arms and a loving heart.
I test you respond
If I give a lead you will fall in the trap.
This tug of war of my soul,
Is a game only I enjoy.
I'll match you step for step.
I'll go toe to toe.
But the second you slip up...
I will know!
This tug-of-war of my soul,
Is a game only I enjoy.

I'm Trying

I'm trying,
I'm not perfect.
I tried to tell you,
I can't do this.
I don't trust and I've been burnt.
You tell me "I won't do that
And you will be fine."
But I have heard that line a hundred thousand
Different times.
I test,
I push,
I could teach a broncho how to buck.
I see pattern changes as red flags.
You keep saying it's okay,
But I just heard that exasperated sigh and you
just Shifted. Just an inch away.
I shut down,
I ball up,
I take vacation in my head and drowned it all
out.
But you can know this without a doubt I'm
trying. I'm trying just for you.

A Best Friend's Prayer of Hope

I can tell when she's been with you,
And the days been good.
She tries to look her best.
I can tell when she's been with you.
She smiles brighter, she's laughing more, and
Talking more, she's hoping and dreaming of
The future again. You make her eyes shine Like
the northern lights.
I can tell when she's been with you,
And the days gone bad.
She makes herself into
The smallest ball,
In the corner of her bed.
I can tell when she's been with you.
She smiles brighter, she's laughing more, and
Talking more, she's hoping and dreaming of The
future again. You make her eyes shine Like the
northern lights.
But she's been here before,
She doesn't trust such happiness.
She won't trust just words.
She sees pattern changes as signs,
Even a tired sigh is a red flag in her mind.
It's not you, don't give up. She is battling herself.

I can tell when she's been with you.
She smiles brighter, she's laughing more, and
Talking more, she's hoping and dreaming of the
Future again. You make her eyes shine like the
Northern lights.
She's lived in darkness for far too long.
She's forgotten how to trust and be loved.
She lived in that darkness
Lying to herself that it was safer.
As she tried to protect her damaged,
Tattered, soul. Her heart's been shattered beyond
Repair.
I can tell when she's been with you.
Her smile's real, she's laughing more, and
talking More, she's hoping and dreaming of the
future again. Life has returned to what was a
darkened shell. Hang in there dear friend. You
make her eyes shine brighter than the northern
lights.

I Caved

I say yes and she says no.
I stand firm but we both know;
One Look, one smile,
One sign of distress, I let it go.

She's the song in my head
That I just can't shake,
She's the smile on my face
That just won't fade.
I may be stubborn as hell,
But when push comes a shove
I'll always side with my girl.

Never thought they'd make
a person patient enough to ever love me. From
the word go I have been a thick-headed fool,
Always going left when I should have gone
right. She just sighs and laughs.
And I'll be damned if that musical sound doesn't
break me down.

I say yes and she says no.
I stand firm but we both know;
One Look, one smile,
One sign of distress, I let it go.

She's the song in my head that I just can't Shake,
She's the smile on my face that just won't fade.
I may be stubborn as hell,
But when push comes a shove,
I'll always side with my girl.

She ain't the first to steal my heart,
Just the one I know won't tear it apart. Feels so
nice to know where I stand.

Woman drives me crazy.
She's so wild and free.
Probably never seen the beaten path a day in her
life. But, she can stop me in my tracks with just
one look.

She makes me laugh so hard it hurts.
She's all the good and my life and none of the
bad. I still can't believe they would make a
person strong enough to love me.

I say yes and she says no.
I stand firm but we both know;
One look, one smile,
One sign of distress, I let it go.
She she's the song in my head that I just can't
Shake,
She's the smile on my face that just won't fade.
I may be stubborn as hell,

But when push comes a shove,
I'll always side with my girl.

I got a temper that would scare the devil himself.
Quick with the fist and no patience to boot. My
mood just as dark. One smile of hers And I'm
filled with sunshine.

The touch of her hand on mine washes it all way.
When I'm with her I feel like I can conquer the
world. I Never thought they'd make a person
brave enough to love me.

I say yes and she says no.
I stand firm but we both know;
One Look, one smile,
One sign of distress, I let it go.

She she's the song in my head that I just can't
Shake,
She's the smile on my face that just won't fade.
I may be stubborn as hell,
But when push comes a shove,
I'll always side with my girl.

She fills my soul with music and love,
Makes me Shine and shimmer like the northern
lights. Some Days I wish I had more to offer her

than this damaged soul of mine. But she swears
she doesn't mind.

She lets me work my broodiness out. Lets me
love Her two little ones as if they were my own.
Some days I don't even need to say a word, and
She's already said my thoughts.

Not in my wildest dreams did I ever believe they
Would make a person who would understand
me.

She she's the song in my head that I just can't
Shake,
She's the smile on my face that just won't fade.
I may be stubborn as hell,
But when push comes a shove,
I'll always side with my own.

New Reality

Tiny hands shake my feet,
Little giggles follow.
Shake the sleep,
Where am I?
Slight shift,
There's an arm around me.
Happy sigh,
It wasn't a dream!
This is my new normal,
A new reality.
Sweet smile,
Warm eyes.
Don't wake me up yet,
If this is a dream!